WHY DUST SHALL NEVER SETTLE UPON THIS SOUL

Why Dust Shall Never Settle Upon This Soul

Poems by

Ryka Aoki

biyuti publishing

Toronto, Canada

Sections of "The Woman of Water Dreams" appeared in different versions in Tandem, Volume II: The Complete Second Season of the Lit Slam (Tandem: Poems of San Francisco's Lit Slam, Volume 2).

A version of "Sometimes Too Hot the Eye of Heaven Shines" first appeared as a chapbook from Inconvenient Press and Radar Publications.

Published by Biyuti Publishing
Toronto, Canada
https://publishbiyuti.org

ISBN: 978-0-9919008-5-5

Cover: Melanie Gillman

This book is printed on acid-free paper.

Acknowledgments

Thank you to Karen Garrabrant, Khary Jackson, Daphne Gottlieb, Robert Morgan, A.R. Ammons, Jean Jenkins, Robert Yehling, K.B. "Tuffy" Boyce, Celeste Chan, Scott Turner Schofield, Michelle Tea, and Justin Chin. Thank you to Askari Gonzalez and nina malaya. Thank you to Roger Gilbert for introducing me to the long poem form. And special thanks to Steph, for her patience as I wrestled with the emotions that went into this volume.

For Alexis and Donna

Contents

Foreword

I debated whether or not to add a foreword to this book. Part of me wants very much to let the poems speak for themselves. But this book represents the end of a long journey for me. It's my first ever book dedicated to poetry, something that I was not sure was going to happen. In fact, up until only a few years ago, I thought it would be impossible. I feel so many emotions right now. It's a lot to process, and I have always processed best on paper, and I feel like I'd like some company along the way.

Poetry is where I have always felt most at home. However, being home has always been complicated. Although I love the idea of being home, home itself was never a safe or viable place. I looked to poetry as an escape from my actual home. And, when somehow I was admitted to the MFA program at Cornell University, I discovered an environment so rarefied and magical that I thought I might finally get away.

Cornell was like nothing I had ever seen, at least in reality. I was stunned by how the faculty lived and worked. With all my heart, I wished for a future life like theirs—with a quiet office, a well-worn desk, a wall of books, a comfy chair and a window overlooking some sort of courtyard or garden. I had no desire to deal with ugliness, with violence. I had no desire to look back on my past. I wanted a locked door with frosted glass. I couldn't even think about justice—I just wanted to leave my childhood home for a newer, quieter, safer one. I wanted an escape. I wanted peace.

Yet being at Cornell was from peaceful. Most of my time I was frustrated, not at my classmates, nor even the interminably cold winters, but at my own inability to become the writer that I felt I had to be—cultured, privileged, and above all, brilliantly safe. Yet, the more that I tried to be that ideal artist, the more I felt that I was missing something vital. Ownership? Self? I felt surrounded by people who knew who they were, their stations, what they wanted to write. Me? Pale imitations all.

More than any other type of writing, I feel that poetry demands truth. There's nothing Hollywood-glamorous about writing a poem. It's clumsy stumbling most of the time, with generous helpings of self-importance and self-pity. But, at least for me, the poem must contain truth. If I'm being evasive, or lying, even unconsciously, the poem reacts. There's nothing like a poem to remind you and where you are.

Even if you don't know yourself.

I returned from Ithaca even more lost and confused. I was back where I started, with my one ticket out of town wasted. There would be no comfy office, no quiet courtyard, no peace. It was over. I most likely would have broken, had not one lucky act saved me: I continued to write poetry. And somehow, my constant probing for what was wrong with my poetry led to finding what was wrong with me. Which finally led me to realize that writing wasn't the only issue I had.

It wasn't until leaving Cornell that I realized all those years of not fitting, of feeling I had the wrong voice, might have been in part because I was transgender. Soon after, my therapist helped me admit to myself that I had been the victim of child abuse. The process was so painful. But it was emancipating, and strengthening.

With new eyes, I looked back at the poems that truly inspired me. Not the names and lifestyles, but the actual words. I realized that my favorite poems did not run away from their pasts—they *transformed* them. After trying to write poetry from a perspective and privilege I never had, I finally stopped trying to be somewhere and someone else. I began to concentrate not on running and escaping my world, but facing and transforming it. My time at Cornell, and even before that, my time home, began to fall into context, producing newfound form and richness. And gradually a type of poetry finally began to come from a hand, heart, and voice I could truly call my own.

In the past, I desired a poetry that offered escape from the pain and nonsensical cruelty of the world. Forget this life; somewhere in chaos of the world, there had to be room for a pastoral, quiet space, where none of the outside mattered.

You can spend lifetimes waiting for a place like that.

Yet are we really interested in poems and poetry that come from such a quiet, bucolic fiction? While at Cornell, one of my professors once said that in the US we kill our poets with kindness. At the time, I thought he was crazy. But after my experiences, I realize his wisdom.

Why do poets seem to rise from places and spaces of oppression? Why do those who hunger for existence, significance, and safety also seem to hunger for verse?

In my hangings-out with other queers of color, I have become familiar with a pattern—one that resonates with my own life—where oppression is more than having nameable obstacles and villains. Life itself becomes the enemy, whether it's planning your trip around a nonexistent gender-neutral bathroom, or taking four hours to run a 20-minute errand because the bus is late. Life itself is oppressive when the only thing that seems to have any regularity are the bills or the insults or the panic attacks that keep you awake every night.

Oppression is the extra pain you feel in your bladder, the sodden feeling you get when someone accuses you of going to McDonald's when it's the only way you can afford to take your kids out for a meal in a place with air conditioning. Oppression reduces conflict and meaning to an impersonality that can pummel a soul until even its existence loses meaning.

For, when society and institutions operate on a statistical scale, where on earth is there room for the personal? What gives the self its significance? At times such as this, it is not the body that most thirsts or hungers, but the soul. We can do far more, if we simply know that we *matter*, that there is significance in who we are, in what we do.

And this is where I finally realized that poetry can sing. Unlike the weightiness of essays or prose, poems can be portable, personal things. Poetry links us not through our shared philosophies or stories, but through the minutiae of our day-to-day existences. A poem can bring seemingly endless stupid impersonal craziness to a personal, human scale and, at least for a while, provide space for contemplation, reflection, perhaps even a little peace.

In "Ars Poetica," Archibald Macleish writes:

"For all the history of grief
An empty doorway and a maple leaf."

One doorway. Not a labyrinth of closed doors. One leaf. Not a forest of lost opportunities. Poetry is one of the few ways we can transform the broadband of oppression into something manageable. It does this by insisting that one's personal experiences, one's personal world, does not merely exist the world—but embodies it. We don't have to measure ourselves against the global or universal; our existences themselves are enough to connect and sanctify us. Poems remind us that we are significant not because of what how much land we own, or how many guns we have, but who we intrinsically are.

This is a world where some children laugh and others are beaten. Where some children are cast out, other blend right in, where some have clean water and bedsheets... Where we force our activists into ignoring their health, our artists to give up before they turn twenty-five. Where people are so addled, so shell-shocked and overwhelmed that they protest their own health insurance. Where there are picnics and beaches and fireflies and even ice cream.

This is the world where poetry most matters, not through its ability to offer escape, but in its ability to transform one's surroundings and link even God and eternity to one's coffee-mug search for a shopping list, significance, and truth.

But here, perhaps, I'll stop and let the poems take over. Thank you so much for listening, for reading, and for being alive.

hug
Ryka

Why Dust Shall Never
Settle
Upon This Soul

The Woman of Water Dreams

1.

Consider
that for every rational number,
there exists an infinite array
of values that do not resolve.

The dead or frightened
housecat. The slipshod dance
of sun and moon. A Shanghai

butterfly splits the baryons
of a faraway nucleus... And you
wonder why I like donuts
a bit too much?

Against infinite
babble, any rational value
is nothing. So nothing
makes sense. Terrifying

to consider this now,
when so many friends have died.

One morning,
a gunman shot up our library.
Killed the groundskeeper
who waved
from the yellow electric car.

For all he was,
he will forever be known
as the groundskeeper.

His daughter was killed as well.
For all she was,
she will always be
known as his daughter.

What is true and proud?
What survives the infinite crush
of hidden, transient, lost?

The murderer
sees you, or no.
The family accepts you, or no.
Your blood test comes
clean, or no.

Who pop-n-locked
with the beautiful men
free-falling past mornings
after, holding
quilts and lovers and ashes—

for what?
A green light too early,
a stutter-step late?
What is life well-lived?
Who fluffs a pillow
through the luck
of a silenced phone?

But that we meant
more in being,
than being wherever we are.

2.

With another November,
the names of trans people
change color and fall.

Mispronounced, sainted,
ceded to anonymous candles,
anonymous flame.

Someone will pledge money.
Someone will start singing.

Some inspired someone will say,
"I think all hatred is bad!
Why can't life just be good
for everyone?"

Past each favorite cousin,
each favorite movie,
each crisp new résumé…
Past each broken heel

fall wax and remembrance
just for a moment
still warm to the touch.

"She was fierce."
"An angel on earth."
"Enchanting."

I smell carne asada,
hear the #4 bus.

The hole in my heart murmurs yes,
yes, yes...

Stunted fathers. Neglected boys.
Cocktails of hormones
in stressed-altered wombs.

Healing the village,
speaking with the dead.
Dancing to the heavens
for fortune and rain.

Blessed goddesses, prophets,
mermaids in rainbow
flags and almost-
tenure-track in the new
Queer Studies Department.

Teeth kicked out, jawbones foot-
stomped into sidewalks.

False lashes and fables
entrance another's ever after.
Lace and illusion entangle the bedpost,

as I rattle my vanity
for foundation, concealer,
a face to a mispronounced name.

3.

She killed herself
the way queer folks do:
Writing of one-horned
aliens, road-rage unicorns…

She killed herself,
the way queer folks do:
Living as role-model, inspiration
to all but what true love knows…

Behind the fishing poles,
there's a Coleman ice chest,
a Lionel train.

A tiny wooden stool with marks
of Crayola and someone's baby
teeth.

I try to pray, yet thirst
only for silence, for sleep.

Lost in the desert, the woman
of water dreams.

Obon, Vigils, Chanukah.

I've learned
we used to be healers.
I've learned
we used to be beloved.

Vigils, Birthdays, Vigils.

Don't know
what else I've learned,
except we know
a lot of dead people.

*Candles, more candles,
more candles, more...*

Be yourself?
Sure! Festoon yourself in sideshow sequins,
thrift-store sex.
The world cums, vomits,
locks its children away.

The sales clerk watches too closely.
Your hometown is not your hometown.

Live without apology?
Sure! Have your life debated by experts
you'll never meet, cast out
by ohana you never knew.

Ask who hides
from family, from womyn,
from the D that the S triggers,
long after the T should be P.

Ask who can visit the supermarket
for orange juice,
salad dressing, and paper towels.

Maybe tomorrow, it will be different.
But today?

Ask why you were born today.

Ask what is good, bad. Ask what is justice.
Ask how eternal truths
should rest so much upon today.

4.

My mother stirs her pot of spareribs
with brown sugar and soy sauce--
with vinegar and regret for a son
who has wasted his life on Lord-knows-what.

No future, no wedding, not even a house...

Steam rises from the stockpot,
like the stories of spices, songs
and all the home this girl will never know

from one who calls gay people "it,"
hearsays immigrants and AIDS,
would disown her firstborn if she knew
what sins her sins had spawned.

That I could tell her how I stir my verse
with Lahaina-girl rhythm.
How in my kitchen, she would know
every pot and pan and spice.

The flesh grows tender. The flavors bind.
Waiting for that moment
just before it burns.

Just before I leave. Just before
another trans woman obliterated
on a Facebook page, or down the street,

or just before my mother's eyes.

Last post on Facebook:
someone misdialed her number
but called her a faggot, anyway.

Last post on Facebook:
we should all remember her by
donating to someone else's
nonprofit transgender study.

What is sacred? What is sure?
It is comforting to declare,
"I have always been me!"

But my friends used to call.
My aunty once held me as I slept.

Run. Fall. Flash back to a beating

as I hold a next drink, next
cigarette, the next stranger's lies
against my tongue.

The phone is ringing. Do I let it go?

Tchaikovsky litters the asylums.
Dickinson rips the wings
off a Lady's Slipper orchid.
Thoreau claws, "Where am I?"
in lungs as flat as unfallen snow.

People I promise to remember
forever change the moment they leave.
And every day before.

5.

Who loved? Who bled? Who
recorded the first
words I said? Who read
to shut my careless eyes?

Who said, before they realized
that I could one day be dead

to them, their world, their prayers,
that they'd be with me
no matter where
I went? When was that message

sent? For I'm not
the same person I was then.
And will never return
to that there and then.

No matter how I may or may
not try:

Release.
Remember.
Goodbye.

6.

Consider
the irrational array
of moments, where
a single rational value
does not resolve.

The cat survives.
The moon recedes.
The sashimi is disgusting,
trendy, delicious, endangered.

People die for what
I am. People insist what I am
has no meaning at all.

Waiting by the windowsill,
with laptop,
a cup of coffee, and a donut,

to be yourself,
you cede yourself
to butterflies, to baryons,
to wind.

And no one to answer,
"Tranquility."

A Song of Someplace Yet to Fall

1.

What can one do
when brilliant friends who remain brilliant
leave?

The Egyptian astrologer, incanting
psalms of forgotten souls.
(Gone)

The space-time composer, with pocket
universe of beat-matched LEDs.
(away)

The enlightenment weaver threading certain
 and unfallen yarns.
(never to look back.)

What can one do
when those who taste prophecy in a teaspoon,
feel symphonies in a Van Nuys cul-de-sac,
hear colors amidst the coldest February grey,

at a pronoun, find nothing
worth another thought?

Grab the mic, cue the karaoke!
What else could this be, but a song?

By now, I was supposed to have
mall-walked to arthritic elder-hood.
Tia Ryka, perched upon padded chair
to speak lovingly

of Arena, Fuck, Fang,
the downtown loft with the best cocaine.
Peanuts, where Sinead O'Connor
hid between an inside wall
and her outside bodyguard.

Of Sin-a-Matic, Illusions,
drag shows at the old Queen Mary.
Cutting lines of hardest house
as the gorgeous ones dance,
or sip vodka tonics,
or give head in lime-green
restroom stalls.

Of how the strobe lights
knew to stop at the makeup and glitter,
to leave us weary as the dead
morning streets when the mocking
birds sang and the battered pickup
trucks came to stack the LA

X-Press kiosks with free tranny ads
to remind us there was someplace
yet to fall.

Never expected to wake
to school boards banning Harper Lee,
evolution as a fad,

sick sisters refusing their meds.
Never expected to have to revisit
the mucus, the wasting, the blindness,
the heart-lung gurgles of struggling
through one last hopeless night—
the guilty final wish that she
would just…die.

Who would have thought survival
might rest upon how long one holds
her melody, her sobriety,
her breath?

2.

Slammed faces, slammed doors,
a cold KFC bucket,
some cole slaw someone
pulled from a dumpster...

"It gets better?"
What does that mean ?

Might Hello Kitty sing?
A mother cry? Would a father
even miss the Disneyland daughter
he hadn't seen since she
was supposed to be his boy?

"We must remember these
transgenders who simply
wanted be themselves."

She was cosmic headscarves,
tapdance fingertips, and origami eyes.

She was satin camisoles,
bedsheet corsets. Flowers, cards,
the hospice lobby for those
too courageous to walk inside.

There was nothing simple
about her, or her, or her,
or her
or her...

Bless those who
disowned their sons, yet say
they listen to the same
punk rock as they always have.

Bless those whose children
fled on a nighttime Greyhound bus,
yet still bake cookies
with raisins instead of chocolate chips.

May God help
those proper Presbyterians
who kicked out their daughters,
whose NPR membership leads to nights
discussing the oppressed
people of the day and how
it's maddening, but not realistic
to demand justice
for another generation or three.

Light a candle. Loop a ribbon.

For in a world without runaways,
castoffs, and queers,
who shall redeem the rope,
the razors, the cans of gasoline?

3.

After life comes death.
After death comes
the Community Memorial.
After the Community Memorial comes
the HIV Questionnaire.

Then some grad student
discards the personal comments
to perform T-tests
on the numbers that remain.

A null hypothesis.
A grant proposal.
A new coffee maker.

Four miles south, bulletproof windows,
2-for-1 Pizza,
Cash 2 Go, $1 Chinese Food.

And the scholars go:

"I am sure I am sure.
So sure that I can assure you for sure
that surely you are not sure
who you are. And the best way to ensure
who you are, I am sure
is for you to be sure you are sure
that until I can be sure you are
sure who you are, you surely can't
be sure you are sure. So don't
say you are sure because surely
I am sure that you can't be sure."

Meanwhile, on the streets it's time
to get authentic and start channeling
"WE-shall-OH-verrr-CO-o-ome…"

Invoke the right Frida, quote
the right Audre

Lorde. To shake things up, to organize,
to close one's eyes, and
righteously fantasize of a favorite
genderqueerish hottie with a dancer's ass,
chestnut thighs, dreads, and high, high
cheekbones.

Auto-tuned, ISO food trucks
Riding day-glo fixies for anarchy and fair trade
Americanos they consume to get real, get hard,
get laid.

Revolution? A blood sport.
Because dead queers are easier to pray to.
Because they don't talk back
and kill the buzz.

Another sodden morning.
Another rent check due.

In another life, someone
skins a plum, frowns,
then spits what clings
too tart and tightly to the seed.

4.

But I am not cruelty-free. I do not offer a gluten-free option.

I won't talk like a pirate. I won't pump up the volume, get wasted, have sex with you at Burning Man. I won't dig your hip-hop, save the planet at this badass rally, talk Chinese, support your Greenpeace, stop eating sushi forsake animal proteins watch Glee ride a fixiedonatetoIndiegogoleggoyourEggo.

I start my Honda, drive
to my favorite freezer section
soft-shoe past the okra and peas,
waltz by the Breyers
Caramel Praline Crunch.

You miss Chik-Fil-A?
I am my own guilty pleasure.

The security guard, the cashier,
even the cart with one stuck wheel
cannot stop the revel
of this nighttime promenade.

Twenty years ago, the astrologer
would not suspend his disbelief.
Ten years ago, the composer
could not harmonize
transgender with friend.
Five years ago the weaver
unraveled a rainbow at my name.

Someday my car
won't pass the smog test.
Just found out I may go blind.
Each day I take five pills
to make me be a little more
like something I can never be.

Someone may mark me
with bad weather and omens.
Judgment might thread through
the foot-treadle stars.

Yet I will hear hummingbirds,
sip my coffee, maybe sit on an ice chest.

Until her saviors go away.
Until her spirit guide stops
reciting every reason to kneel
before the next muscle
car blowing down her street,

who can ponder which witch
she has become,
yet how completely she still
would give her dance to love?

5.

To pull a sweater from my closet,
shove my cell phone in my purse,
then march for groceries
with a five-minute stop at CVS?

The composer
may abandon his backbeat,
the astrologer may withhold
his gaze. The weaver
may sever the threads of youth,
threads of self—even as she cuts
another inconvenient thread,

unable to grasp
why dust shall never settle
upon this soul.

After a Lifetime of Saving the World

1.

We scan the farmer's market
for the crispest apples.

It is the season for apples.

Three blocks west, someone's
dressed like Tinker Bell, posing
with a couple from Spokane
in front of Grauman's Chinese Theatre.

A snap, a smile.
Another sweet moment,
another dollar made.

Even here,
we glean the seasons by smell.

Next door loquats,
roadtrip cherries,
backyard peaches,

Anjou pears. My mother's
three bags of shiny persimmons
in the patio.

I have friends who insist
there are no seasons in LA.

Let them.

Let them seize the imperatives
the correlations,
communities, the arithmetic
of greater numbers.

Let each equation
be more compelling than the last.

Let glitter bedazzle death and angels.
What is passed over will be there,

always. Past starlings and storefronts
and the color of home,

let them prophesy all the time
in the world.

Fuck time's delicacy.
Fruit does not spoil as long
as it's forbidden.

2.

A philosopher once asked if I believe in God.

My friend lost two friends
and one of them was
my friend; so was another,
and in the morning,

I could kiss you, not to wake
you, but to linger a little, resting
a bit where my nose still brushed
your neck, and yes
I was crying, because you stirred,
and smiled and we were
going shopping and it was still
not even May.

A philosopher once asked if I believe in God.

I said, "No, I have experience."

And so, even now,
I can disbelieve all I want, but I shall always know

that I would want another night
next to you, breathing, dancing on byways,
no matter how afraid.

Up overhead, we peered
at what snuggled the side
of a Griffith Park ravine,
We identified it with an app
you downloaded from a cloud,
then snipped a sprig

of Showy Evening Primrose
to dream of planting
in our someday backyard,
at least until the allergies set in.

3.

I am writing a speech
to tell a group of earnest undergrads
something hopeful and life-affirming.

How does one say, "Trim just a bit of
flesh. The glass slipper will fit—
you'll get to the ball, dance with the prince?"

Feet blister, mouths bleed rubber and cum,
the backbeat fades to cross-
referenced, cross-gendered graves.

Jeezus... She was only 22...

You shhh me, say,
"It's 4 a.m., and you'll be awake
when you are."

In the come and go of neutrinos,
housecats, a sweetheart's note
and schoolyard beating,

there is not enough courage in my hand
but for the courage I hold in yours.

What beatifies leftover lo mein?
Styrofoam? Chopsticks,
plastic forks, two napkins, three

packs of crappy
soy sauce neither of us will use?

You slog home drenched in empty,
from work you swear you only do
for the money, though
we both know otherwise.

Rent's increasing 4.5%.
LA wants $61.42 in taxes we don't owe.

What trip to Paris?
We're hoping to visit
the supermarket between paychecks.

Leftovers for the wok, the stockpot.
Leftover rice, leftover bok choy.

Yesterday, I yearned for when
I could buy a bag of salad
without caring how quickly
even the freshest greens spoil.

Yesterday, I yearned for clean dishes,
a clean refrigerator.

But yesterday, I could tell you
how someone waited a little longer
to hold the elevator door,

how the Walgreens clerk heard
me sniffle, and said,
"I hope you feel better."
or the helpful woman
at the Post Office saying, "Oh, people
forget the postal rates all the time!"

And today,
as I entered the liquor store,
an actor rushed past me to buy lemon drops
then dashed to the theatre next door.

I bought a two-liter of Diet Coke,
three cans of sardines in tomato sauce,
and stammered "kam sab ni da"
to the shop owner
who knew I said it wrong,
yet smiled, and nodded
completely
and simply to me.

4.

One can forge documents,
reinvent identities, concatenate
acronyms,

be lost in our flags, our labels,
our unfilled prescriptions and
lists of the dead.

Though the cure for cancer
may not cure cancer,
or suicide, or a trip to the doctor,

who will whisper, "I'll go with you,
be scared with you,
trust what you say,
and always be here?"

When two-spirits peer into moonless
native sky. When transsexuals primp
for conjugal visits with surgeon
and syringe.

When I'm writing how even as she ended,
someone always made sure her nails
were absolutely perfect,

who turns off my phone,
closes my laptop, gets a popsicle
to ease my a sore throat?

Who we are? What is that?
I think? I am? What is that,
but in all that I give

I am yours.
I am yours.
I am yours.

Build with me.
Walk with me.
Grow old and tired and
share supper with me.

And with you I light a candle.
And with you I reheat the noodles.
Or so we hope
we hope
when we are weak
we can say we know
what it feels like
to truly love.

♥

Today, a sparrow was perched
on the banana tree,
so the hummingbirds were (probably)
         too frightened to land.

And near the galaxy's core,
a black hole stripped a pearl-
blue star into ribbons of fire and poetry
is all one has strength to hear

when we don't have enough daylight
to waste even a little food:

Leftovers go to stir-fry,
stir fry becomes soup,

and soup is what a lover needs
after a lifetime of saving the world.

No More Hiroshimas

To the members of the American Society of Hiroshima-
Nagasaki A-Bomb Survivors, who have dedicated their lives
to promoting compassion, peace, and love.

爪

In reality,
to speak of terrible things
does not make
terrible go away.

The air is yet too
raw. For water,
the stones yet beg.

Bare feet, bare sky.
An airplane bringing
nighttime with day.
Cicadas, angels,
flames.

What rests upon the pillowcase?
Another white hair.
Another plane to board.
Pika-Don!

How bright the song of ashes!
How easy are angel's wings!
How does one foul moment
find so many souls to burn…

Sisters, classmates, the man
who brought fresh fish.

Of lost hair, lost tears,
lullabies and strips of skin—

to cry of our loss,
is it really so brave?
It is only nature, when one is hurt,
to scream.

心

"No more War!
No more Hiroshimas!"

In reality,
to speak of terrible things
does not make terrible go away.

So who are we
on a clear morning
like this one?
As we tell these children

of all we should not
have seen, nor heard,
nor smelled, nor been—

to dance anew with fireflies,
a freshest peach before it falls?

夂

What lights upon
this beautiful world?

On a clear morning
like this one:

A father flies a kite.
His daughter's voice
is bright and clear as tea.

"No more War!
No more Hiroshimas!"

Even barefoot. Even now.
Where angels
should not follow.
Where bombs
should never fall.

Where airplanes
only dreaming
should dare
pretend to fly.

Sometimes
Too Hot the Eye of
Heaven Shines

Prologue

On Santa Monica and Vermont,
the sky pours violet as a million girls
named Maria spill masa and hominy
from an orange Number 4 unto a deluge
of white cars and blue, diving
left against waves of yellow-turning-red.

A green baby bottle, half-full of apple juice,
con Dora la Exploradora, lolls on its side.
The mija in the indigo stroller slips away, just
in time to miss Dora waving goodbye.

Sometimes Too Hot
the Eye of Heaven Shines

1.

God grants gifts, speaks Common Sense—
that His gifts are to His Glory, all to Him.

Tonight, I'm scrounging
for cash-price only gasoline, not seeing
American flag wheelchair guy glancing
as I glance off the 101—
and in all God's Glory,
I'll hit that same damned pothole
I prayed to never hit again.

I was born in the Queen of Angels,
but am never without a Thomas Guide.
You cannot receive these streets by GPS—
laces of boulevards converge
where road work blocks access,
and only a right-turn donut shop
can be where you were going
but could never find alone.

2.

Someone said that there's no there there.
But the city moves so fast, you see it only
if it decides to love you, too.

I cannot explain any clearer than where I'll be
when the road construction stops,
the light rail is built, and every migrant worker
understands that sleeping within train tracks
does not protect you from snakes.

And every East Coast transplant understands
that migrant workers brave far worse
than snakes or trains, or even sleep.

3.

Someone asks if Hollywood shines at night.
I say Hollywood shines brightest afterhours,
when an underage skirt makes the sidewalk
speak in tongues.
When a bacon-wrapped hot dog spits
at the streetsweeper with a Sunday School voice.
When a needle jabs Sh'ma Yisroel
into a queer punk tweeker's neck
while his father faps to BarebackTwinks.com
a thousand shivas away.

4.

Someone dreams of rain,
of reservoirs feathered with dead gulls and salt.
Of sinkholes, highway cones,
four cars spinning, one upside down.

Someone dreams of genius
slamming flash flood triolets
upon a march of ivory palisades.
I ask God for a filthy toilet.
Behind two panes of bulletproof,
the station man glares
not giving a sit or shit what King Lear said...

Soaking in Shakespeare, how sharper
than a serpent's tooth is a child waiting
for the gift of magic words!

5.

My city raises its dead without fanfare or notice.
As prophets blow lepers in the back row of the Tomkat,
a flight of lost pashminas is lilting free from clouds.
Four blocks from a working streetlight,
a tranny ho with green eyes and a hint of mango
calls long distance from a public phone.
My city wakes at 3 a.m.
finally knowing what it forgot to be.

6.

Beneath backfire and bullets,
an unsmoked cigarette sanctifies a vacant lot.
A boxcar labors from Terminal Island
barge to big rig to market
before the silken threads of morning
seduce the last non-planetary star.

7.

Lurching over the Tejon Pass,
fair from fair hauls frozen beef
to a butcher who lives for steel on bone.
I pray with eighteen wheels, descending
unto a four-level interchange
too jammed to navigate or even move.

My Lord, where hope and verses
sway like meat untrimmed,
You see only that I am late. You, who would
rather grind flesh than meet my eyes—
You will draw Your hands across Your apron,
and the bloody residue of Your day
shall witness why I have failed You
yet again.

8.

My father brags I've never worked a day
he couldn't work harder.
He's never seen me work a drunken muse,
his dead-rat cock,
three fingers up his ass, gagging
on his stinky couplets, moaning
when he hits me, and hits me,
and hits me...

9.

Child, I shall never compare you
to a summer's day.
Sister, I do not commute by Gold Line or Red.
I do not park my Honda overnight, in an indoor lot,
with car wash, security, and valet.
Brother, I abuse a substance from which I never wake.
Restless and wandering, when the Black Lite closes,
I chase the dragon in a strange and cold backseat.
Father, the sunrise writhes in the rearview
like the anonymous poet
to whom I kneel and confess I have no friends...
Beside the Western off ramp—
sirens, helicopters, drivers waving *over here, babe.*
Mother, I won't come home tonight
for I am only junk mail and a lost credit card
without the lights, camera, action.

I stumble into a kitchen
blessed with cockroaches and half
a bean burrito, to a bedroom
where loneliness is a stifle of dirty laundry—
last night's inspiration,
a cum stain seeping in the floor.

10. *Queen of Angels*

Old men once declared City Hall
the tallest building by law.
While you hid me from social workers,
asphalt and steel scrambled in cloverleaf exodus
to dreams of three churches
a drugstore and a damned good Chinese take out.

Since you say I lack a center. I will say I have no center.
I agree, not because I have no self, because
even when I believed you, I felt the headlights
in the donut shop where the short man making strudel
let a stranger use the bathroom
that said "Employees Only" in big red letters
that in his personal divinity,
he decided to ignore.

It is your choice; it is not your choice.
It is what you want; it is not what you want.

Rush hour Hummers dilate my veins,
but a deeper traffic flows
as virgin buildings rise like glass anemones
when the mother tide shields them
from fathers and eternal sun.
What I say and what I believe are no longer the same—
I say what I hear, and what I hear is not me.

911 thighs do not bleed for lack of skyline.
Pho 79 has broken no one's eardrum or arm.
I say what I say not because I am weak.
I bear pushcarts and underpasses, even as you
fade in front of the TV.

I sprawl not from squalor,
but when so-called firmament forsakes
my foundations, each precious avenue
may hold the one way to escape.
In the brushfire, or the flood,
or the earthquake, or the drought—
wherever each stop sign wishes to fly, in my expanse
I shall shelter my bruised and brilliant children.
I shall shelter them all.

11.

The neighbor's dog hears the temblor come
but can only bark, as God's image on the onramp
preaches in a ribbed wifebeater
branding freeways with spray paint and sharpie
like a broken son of Cain.

When the Valley fractures at the crosswalk iglesia,
and TV signals hurl bottles at gated satellites,
an old Hmong woman rides a tricycle—
plastic bags of vegetables, all edible,
even as the city riots for the stillness of a distant shore.

12.

The city holds me like a gutter to the sea
as I pray for a sign
to stuff my words in a garbage bag.
For flu season to still me on a Thursday afternoon.
For rose-scented Agua Santa to burst from
La Iglesia de Nuestra Señora Reina de los Angeles
blessing all of us like the animals before Easter—
for cupping the forepaws of animals and angels.
For why the hell is this blindness cured? For why I cry
without shame when queer kids and stray cats
dream of something other
than dying beautiful. For my ugliness, failure,
the 3 o'clock elotero slathering hot corn with butter
and I have no coins for laundry.
For every blessed night
in a K-Town supermarket I spend alone
because you retch at filefish and garlic.

Please God,
I pray that one day sweet railcars
will swing low upon magnetic tracks,
that no one dies with an empty pocket and a ringing phone,
that I can ride an eastbound bus and understand
why you write me in a language that burns gasoline.

Praise God, gracias, kam'sa'eyo
for the gifts that a dollar in quarters,
a City of Angels, and a freeway,
illuminated by whatever dreams I have,
can bring.

Epilogue

Wednesday morning. Nine-oh-five.
Just outside my window, the leaf blower
is strapped to a young father I wish
I could smile for, but that my lazy ass is still in bed.
My car's the only one covered in the dust
and not in a day-job parking lot.

Near the 101 onramp. Nine-oh-five.
the leaf blower sounds too much like
other motors.
I despise the sound of motors—
Beemers, Escalades, that damned Prius,
an eighteen wheeler and its engine brake,
a greasy Datsun pickup with three grown men
and a mattress—each conveying so much more
than the part-time teacher with the Honda
whose first act of the day
shall be to kill a cockroach
that ignores her in the bathroom sink.

In the next room, my degree hides in a box on a shelf,
and all my shelves stow books
which I have read and even understand.
Which haven't given me a clue
why I'm still in Los Angeles, why?

You're missing direction. Missing a center.
Irvine has a new PF Chang's. Your cousin
is a dentist with a Lexus and a daughter named Marissa.

I am full of missing.
I am full of day-old bread, MGD, and cheap soju.

I can't leave while I'm
choking on the stubble
of the over five hours of sleep
I'm supposed to be so lucky to have—

I can't anything. I can't get selected for a jury.
I can't stop a caffeine headache or a leaf blower
blowing the same crap up and down.
Another God is with us. Emanuel. Whatever. Amen.

And that would be me—
stirring myself to a scoop
of instant coffee, a noise on the radio,
pencils as dull as thought, drooling at my Mac
like a yoga teacher strung on patchouli
and a Youtube of a fucking cat
chasing a felt mouse with a goddamned jingly bell...

Forgetting that I was teaching until 10 p.m.
the night before,
my car the last one home.
That I teach night school because
I have no one to come home to, because
I planned it this way, even hours after I log off Skype
to jingle how much I love this city,
where I have to shove four trash bins
to clear enough space to park and gush
that golly-gee the Salvadoreños on the corner serve
the best grilled breakfast sandwich in the world...

But I am going back to sleep—
where my therapist says
all good things lay, to not believing
salvation comes wrapped in a suicide note
with a side of fries and an extra-large Diet Coke.

Centerless,
I am free to both sleep
and stroll down Fairfax from Ethiopians to Jews
to Koreans and queers and on each corner a 7-11
and someone standing next to the double glass door.

Without direction,
I breathe each boulevard, street, lane, road, avenue, way—
You say I'm wasting time, and I have
believed You, in part, even until now.
I do not know, but that I cannot fly—
That heaven shines unbearable.
And in not flying, I can only drive,
and behind each pair of eyes behold another light.

Living so near the 101, the morning
motors condemn me, and farther away
a fish truck from Chinatown unloads
ice chest tilapia to a Mexican deep fryer,
and closer, the leaf blower
sputters purple maledictions through my building...

But I am going back. Screw the leaf blower,
the LED billboard with the
can't-be-real-no-fair Persian swimsuit model—
I have soft green earplugs, thick curtains
a satin facemask from Bed Bath and Beyond.
Because I have been working
'till 10 p.m., and even on nights off and long after
I have been driving my Honda to find eternal lines
to time like what Whitman said he found
and Eliot said was *not*.

On boulevards divided,
as spotlights catwalk on movie theater clouds
I covet a runaway pair of shiny rhinestone shoes.
Waltzing not to love songs,
nor what voyeurs might assume,
to dream, perchance, to sleep.
For even without center, I follow
what my city has told me all along:

I may be the last to leave. But I shall be
by far the latest to return.
And wherever, whatever gives this life,
it is not in the late night K-town Pho house,
but that next Tuesday I will eat there, not in the 101,
but that I shall once more drive its length, not
in "I love you,"
but that I can on some days hear it, and hold it
and in holding it, have the strength to let the morning
to thee, the Queen of Angels, go.

RYKA AOKI has been honored by the California State Senate for "extraordinary commitment to free speech and artistic expression, as well as the visibility and well-being of Transgender people." She earned her MFA in Creative Writing at Cornell University, and is the recipient of a University Award from the Academy of American Poets, and is the author of He Mele A Hilo, and Seasonal Velocities. She is a professor of English at Santa Monica College and of Queer Studies at Antioch University.

Please visit: www.rykaryka.com.

Cover artist **Melanie Gillman** is creator of "As the Crow Flies," which has been nominated for the Slate Cartoonist Studio Prize and an Eisner Award.
Please visit: www.melaniegillman.com

biyuti publishing is a small, independent publisher founded, managed, and run by trans women of colour. This title, and others, can be found at https://publishbiyuti.org.

CPSIA information can be obtained
at www.ICGtesting.com
Printed in the USA
FSHW011312101220
76780FS